Poetic Views
of
Life

Laurie Wilkinson

This edition published in Great Britain in 2014 by

MyVoice Publishing
33-34 Mountney Bridge Business Park
Westham
PEVENSEY
BN24 5NJ

Copyright © Laurie Wilkinson 2014

The right of Laurie Wilkinson to be identified as the author of this work has been asserted by him in accordance with the Copyright, Designs and Patents Act 1988.

All rights reserved. No part of this publication may be reproduced, transmitted, or stored in a retrieval system, in any form or by any means, without permission in writing from the publisher, nor be otherwise circulated in any form of binding or cover other than that in which it is published and without a similar condition being imposed on the subsequent purchaser.

ISBN 978-1-909359-30-7

Cover Photo: The Spectacular Victoria Falls rainbow
Photo by the author.

Acknowledgements

I would like to thank my wife, Iris, for her help and support, and also my family and friends for their encouragement. Many thanks also to Anderida Writers group in Eastbourne Sussex for their positive comments, feedback and advice so crucial for the confidence required to compile this completed work. I would also like to express my gratitude to My Voice Publishing for the opportunity and guidance with the publishing process.

Lastly and by no means least, thanks to the reader for your interest and even more to anyone buying this book who will ensure that a donation from sales will go to the charity Help for Heroes.

Poetic Views of Life

Laurie Wilkinson

Introduction

I enjoyed the written word from an early age and often expressed myself by writing, increasingly as I got older. During the 1990's I had articles published in the Nursing Press and in 2001 I completed a degree in mental health and realised that I had enjoyed the writing challenges required to complete it.

About that time I started writing poems according to my emotions and then quite recently I got positive feedback and encouragement regarding my poetry, which motivated me to write more poems on my opinions, observations and outlook on life. This book is the result.

Laurie Wilkinson Bsc (hons) RMN

Aspects and Feelings

Life's wonder is all around us
However near or far we look,
So I have made poetic observations
And put them in a book.

Romance will touch and thrill us,
Tragedy can make us cry
While humour lifts our spirits,
Reflection questions why?

Everyone has needs and feelings
Should they run off and retire,
But knowing views of others
Just may switch on and inspire!

Poetic Views of Life

Laurie Wilkinson

Contents

Acknowledgements	I
Introduction	III

ROMANCE

Unknown Journey	3
Dancing Light	4
Bubble	5
Safeway	6
Laughing Sadness	7
Contradiction	8
Headlight	9

HUMOUR

Bear in the Window	13
Bar Room Star	15
Yoga	16
Jade	17
Idle Concern	18
Benefit of Laughing	19
Cassie	21
Travelling Bears	22

REFLECTIVE

Diamonds For Worms	25
Wandering Within	26
The Friend	27
Tainted Babes	28
Past Echoes	29
Silence Thunders	30
Monsoon	31
Ghouls	32
Hand of God	33

V

Poetic Views of Life

TRAGEDY

Moving On	37
Blind Alleys	38
Out of Time	39
Groom and Doom	41
Crowded Out	43
Speedy End	44
Paradox of Life	45
Miss Judas Regrets	46
Someone Says Goodbye	48
Appendix	51

Laurie Wilkinson

ROMANCE

Poetic Views of Life

Laurie Wilkinson

Unknown Journey

The very beauty of the gift
Was that it was not seen or showing,
We did not know or notice
That something great was growing.

You sailed in your ship, I in mine,
No other course was charted.
We journeyed on across our seas
Unaware just what had started.

I did not know but I looked for you,
Your way, your eyes, your smile.
A touch can take our breath away
And be felt from near a mile.

But the greatest star was yet to shine
Beaming light from sky to sea.
I was manic, laughing , flying
When you said you cared for me!

--ooOoo--

Dancing Light

A dancing light to a room you are
Not seen at once but bright,
Your natural warmth is subtle too
Stronger still with frequent sight.

You are like the solid honest firs
That pretty flower to the moon,
Your laugh and fun could melt a stone
And cause sound minds to swoon.

I could be as your fantasy
Like a moth drawn to a lamp,
As others chase to be near you
Their joy tears running damp.

You may not know you radiate
This warm attracting haze,
Upon unsuspecting people met
Drawn in by your carefree gaze.

A dancing light to a room you are
That embraces all around,
To reach and skip in places dire
Where joy is seldom found.

--ooOoo--

Laurie Wilkinson

Bubble

I cannot see or touch it

This bubble of your love.

But I know now that I need it,

Like the manna from above.

For if I step outside it,

I feel a stabbing pain,

That cuts and hurts my being,

Until I step inside again.

--ooOoo--

Safeway

Go safely as you make your way

Your worth is hard to measure,

Not everyone will value you

But you really are a treasure.

Go safely as you make your way

Turning many a mile and bend,

Strong and sure in knowledge now

You have a special friend!

--ooOoo--

Laurie Wilkinson

Laughing Sadness

Coco pop the circus clown
Had a sadness in his heart,
But he could never show this
He had to play his part,
In a world of joy and laughter
That he would never feel,
So he clapped, laughed and chortled
Though none of it was real.

The world had played a nasty trick
On the clown called Coco pop,
For in love he was a failure
And with women he would flop,
Despite his best intentions
To woo the ladies off their feet,
He never got a second chance
To feel their rumba beat.

Through tear streaked eyes he smiled
At every trick and joke,
That his act demanded of him
Although it all felt like a yoke,
Upon his saddened heart strings
That he never would hear play,
A joyous loving chorus
So a lonely man he'd stay!

--ooOoo--

Poetic Views of Life

Contradiction

Laughing, smiling happy soul
Pure contentment's all you've got,
Until you take a closer look
And see in fact it's not.

Behind the easy ready smile
A mask conceals what's true,
And betrays a deeper inner ache
That belies the outer you.

So it's no lie that makes you laugh
And lights your outer glow,
It's a natural pull to get away
From scenes best not to know.

But still you sail on constantly
Making happy waves and wakes,
To do the deeds required from you
Whatever pain it takes.

And thus your spiral turns and twists
And pulls you up and down,
And mocks your steadfast attitude
To look without a frown.

So now your battle rages on
Unseen and yet severe ,
While you give aid and comfort
To anyone that's near.

Laughing, smiling happy soul
Who wants freedom like a bee,
To be stroked and brought to life
By the special ones that see.

Laurie Wilkinson

Headlight

I have observed you much of late

You may have felt my looking stare,

Perhaps you knew the reason why

Or merely how you seemed to care.

Whilst others queued to build my load

You saw I walked a lonely road,

Rejection can taste an acid pill

That even survivors blood will spill.

So when light invades consuming dark

Flames can rise from a smallest spark!

--ooOoo--

Poetic Views of Life

Laurie Wilkinson

HUMOUR

Poetic Views of Life

Laurie Wilkinson

Bear in the Window

The teddy bear was hanging
by it's neck inside the shop,
So I walked right in to tell them
that I had to make it stop.

A woman came to serve me
and I pointed out their fault,
That a teddy bear was suffering
and by it's neck was caught.

I really did not like to see it
and little kids would be dismayed,
To see that such a cuddly toy
was so callously displayed.

I again told them the problem
and in a shop for charity,
A bear suspended by it's neck
was not very nice to see!

Trying to use some humour
and to get right to the nub,
I told them I was chairman
of the "Bears protection club"

The woman looked quite shaky
and could tell that I was right,
That in a shop front such as this
should not be a grisly sight.

A manager was called to see me
from a room right out the back,
And very soon agreed with me
that she could get the sack,

For not seeing the situation
and the teddy bear's upset,
And very quickly released him
saying she was in my debt!

Then starting from tomorrow
she would change the shop around,
Ensuring that all teddy bears
would then be safe and sound.

If there's a morale to this story
it's that we must learn to care,
For each and every one of us
starting with our teddy bear!

--ooOoo--

Laurie Wilkinson

Bar Room Star

Every pub or place will have one
There are lots of them about,
And while everyone likes talking
He feels the need to shout.

Amongst his group of cronies
He must be the loudest bloke,
Then burst into raucous laughter
Every time he cracks a joke!

I turn my head to see him
But you couldn't miss the noise,
For he's the best at shouting
In the group of loud old boys.

We will all laugh at something
In our own personal way,
Within the bounds of reason
As appropriate for the day.

But this loud man doesn't realise
His grating voice won't nestle,
And he clearly has forgotten
The saying of the empty vessel.

So the loud mans noise continues
And his voice you couldn't douse,
Though I have a deep suspicion
That at home he's like a mouse!

Poetic Views of Life

Yoga

To perform yoga is intriguing
So try it if you dare,
You sit, or lay upon a mat
And puzzle what goes where!

And when you have successfully,
Tied yourself up quite a lot,
Not moving, so it's hard to see,
If you're still alive or not?

But to help you with your yoga
And some of the pain relieve,
You lie very calm and silent,
While you still attempt to breath.

Try another skill of balance
Up on one leg, and smile,
Just practice you can do it,
But it may take quite a while!

There are though, other postures
When you just lay back and rest,
And after all the spasms,
You will like this bit the best.

Lay back and check your breathing
Going slowly in and out,
Surprisingly you feel good
And so relaxed without a doubt.

For those ancient yoga masters
Must have known just what to do,
About being calm and supple,
And living on past ninety two!

Laurie Wilkinson

Jade

To the Devonshire I'll go
For some beer and a linger,
And possibly get served
By Jade and her pointy finger.

She always smiles a greeting
Whoever's at the bar,
So you're sure of a welcome
By the biggest smile by far.

Some girls try oh so hard
To be glam around the place,
But you don't have to try hard
When you have a lovely face!

Most women think that all men
Want a girl with flashing thighs,
But a woman's more attractive
With a grin and laughing eyes.

Even better if she can
Talk of life and normal things,
Without air or presumption
For common men or kings.

So to complete the picture
Of a smashing girl called Jade,
Who without a massive effort
Is a blooming great barmaid!

Idle Concern

The lazy man will flourish
On the back of others work,
The more he sees you labour
The harder he will shirk.

Saying he doesn't mind work,
That he's not scared to graft,
At any hard task or effort,
But at that I only laughed!

So he leaves it all to others
to meet the daily task,
He will just never help out
Whoever dares to ask.

I wonder just how he gets by
Without ever breaking sweat,
for without a doubt he is one
Of the most idle men I've met.

It seems there is no justice
When we all pull our weight,
As this lazy fellow stands there
Just leaning on the gate.

He just has no real intentions
Of giving help to me or you,
And will be inert forever
Whatever we say or do.

But life has a way of sorting
The scales of fair returns,
So when we get our pensions
He will only have concerns!

Laurie Wilkinson

Benefit of Laughing

Laughter rings across the room
Then there's shouts and cheers,
I look towards the revellers
Surrounded by their beers.

It is great to hear the laughing
Silence bettered by the noise,
So I smile back at the cheering
And the grown up girls and boys.

But something doesn't seem right
The laughter's much too fake,
It seems like a competition
And to shout for shouting sake.

Then the raucous noise is louder
By some banging on the table,
And each person sitting round it
Talks as loud as they are able.

If you didn't look too closely
At the total lack of grief,
You wouldn't see their fatness
Or distinctive lack of teeth.

What is this place I've come to?
It just does not seem the same,
As other pubs I've been to
So I will note the name!

A visit out to the toilets
Leaves me a bit perturbed,
Two men talk loudly at me
And I can't make out a word!

Poetic Views of Life

They seem to be quite happy
When they stagger out the door,
And roll towards their table
But one collapses on the floor.

This brings more fits of laughter
Though the bloke looks in distress,
But the revellers don't notice
That he's now a beer soaked mess.

On returning from the toilet
I have a look around the room,
At smaller groups of people
Sitting quietly as the tomb.

So I think I've got the answer
To the revellers all at play,
And their cause for celebration
Is that it is benefits pay day!

--ooOoo--

Laurie Wilkinson

Cassie

Lovely Cassie with the "blondie" hair
I always love it when you are there,
Your warming smile cheers my soul
Even when my team can't score a goal.

You always laugh and joke with vigour
That won't distract me from your figure,
For a girl who laughs with a sense of fun
And looks good too, is a special one.

You buzz round the bar in a happy way
And always find nice things to say,
But your smile hides feelings black as ink
And you won't say exactly what you think.

Lovely Cassie with the "blondie" hair
I always love it when you are there,
We laugh away and joke as friends
But some don't know just where it ends,
And seek to push your fun too far
Forgetting that although a bar,
And their beer money you collect
You and your job deserve respect.

The pubs code says you must wear black
But you could look good dressed in a sack,
And I'd like to see you made up bright
So with some luck perhaps I might!

Poetic Views of Life

Travelling Bears

Ted is a travelling bear
And he has a passport too,
He loves to travel all around
So will come with me or you.

Beth, she is Ted's girlfriend
And they are never far apart,
Since Ted found her abandoned
Now they're joined by teddy hearts.

When going about by aircraft
They go in hold bags snug,
For if carried to the cabin
They may be searched for drugs.

Ted says he has heard stories
Of teddies made to hide,
So custom staff were searching
To see what they had inside.

Beth gets quite upset by this
And starts to fret and shake,
For the fear of being cut apart
Is more than she can take.

So the bears much prefer a car
For their travel if they can,
And on a ferry or the open road
The world outside they scan.

Sitting on the luggage bags
In the backseat without cares,
They reflect on their happy life
Being lucky travelling bears!

Laurie Wilkinson

REFLECTIVE

Poetic Views of Life

Laurie Wilkinson

Diamonds For Worms

(Remembrance Day Green on Blue Killing in Afghanistan 2012)

You wear the colours and guise of friend
So no early grave for me to send,
For I have been sent out here to help
Whilst your medieval country can only whelp,
And all those here that kill, rape, and stone
Are masquerading as your own.
So what have you got to fear from me
When your own tormentors are still free?

But I see a cowards look in your eye
And a Judas covenant is now nigh!
And so you turn your gun on me
Your ill bred eyes that cannot see,
Without my help your sad tragic land
Will only sink beneath the sand,
And you will drown in ten thousand tears
Caused by your brothers equality fears!
I hope you rot, skulking in the night
You're a worm, and my diamond shines bright!

--ooOoo--

Poetic Views of Life

Wandering Within

I have been to another place
Crossed the line and dared to see,
What other shapes and pictures there
Would have in store for me.
But when you start to wander off,
Turn from the beaten track,
You may return from another path
And are never truly back.
It's hard to tell when you go away
If you come back to the start,
For you can be around in flesh
But not with all your heart.

So in the small hour of the dark
And eerie sounds of dawn,
Ghostly figures, words and thoughts
Emerge to mock and fawn.
Are you happy and at hearts rest
Not to change the things that past,
And would you still be where you are
After your choice is cast?
But hindsight is a wondrous thing
It can make all gambles right,
So we must make our peace within
Without the gift of second sight!

--ooOoo--

Laurie Wilkinson

The Friend

Strong is the friend who stands by you
When others turn aside
The minute they're asked to help
They are off to run and hide.

True is the friend who stands by you
In times of your demise,
Always there to chat and cheer
And make sense of all the lies.

Humble is the friend who stands by you
And can't see what he's done
By being right alongside you
With no thought to cut and run.

Loyal is the friend who stands by you
Even if he feels you're wrong,
And tries to mediate a deal
To leave you standing strong.

Caring is the friend who stands by you
When all blows up in your face,
Then will resolve and tend your hurt
And play down the disgrace.

What have you done to earn this friend
Who shelters from the fame?
I suspect that when he was down
You stood by him just the same!

Tainted Babes

Herod has given up his sword
He used to butcher babes,
Now the babes strap on their bombs
They use to butcher men.
What grotesque cause sanctions this?
To turn worlds upside down,
And cannot learn a cowards act
Wont bring a victors crown!

--ooOoo--

Laurie Wilkinson

Past Echoes

There is a tear-drop on the table
From the whispers of the past,
For all the dreams and plans
That somehow did not last.

Despite all, you've emerged now
Out from those mists of time,
Saw the rivers that contained you
And the hills you could not climb.

So you made your way regardless
Of the pitfalls and the traps,
And settled in your castle
With scarce a dip or lapse.

Maybe your destiny is different
From what you'd hoped it would be,
But looking back from now
At that time you could not see
Without the gift of foresight
Just how everything would end.
So thoughts of could've, should've
Are now just scars to mend.

Of course it could be different
From how it's all turned out,
Knowing then just what would happen
We would succeed without a doubt.
But life never is that simple
When the answers can be seen,
So we would make new errors
After the old ones we redeem.

Silence Thunders

Silence echo's loud as thunder
Like the voice of someone dear,
That you will never see again
Or feel their body near.

Silence echo's loud as thunder
In the rooms inside your home,
Where every noise will tell you
That you are all alone.

The special one has gone now
So won' be heard to speak,
Or let you kiss and touch them
And so your eyes will leak.

It's said you don't miss someone
Until after they're not there,
The gift is gone completely
So your life is really bare.

Silence echo's loud as thunder
Even if you are sincere,
So no future substitution
Can ever fully cheer.

There's silence in the heart
Like a thunder in the ears,
And so that silent thunder
Haunts your future years!

Laurie Wilkinson

Monsoon

Pouring, soaking, drenching rain
Descends on us again and again,
Flooding, drowning, spraying wet
Day after day is all we get.

Pounding, crashing, driving wind
Hitting us as though we'd sinned,
Blowing, gusts, and shrieking bluster
So a sigh is all we can muster.

Pouring, soaking, drenching rain
Pounding crashing, a driving force.
Flooding, blowing, drowning storm
Batters us which ever the course.

The wind then drops to just a gasp
And after the sunshine shows,
So when we feel like peering out
Another deluge freely flows.

Gusting wind, and driving rain
Twin partners in their crimes,
Get together to unleash on us
The very worst of times.

Houses flooded, power lines down
Wonder if we'll freeze or drown,
Railways stopped, roads under water
Seems we've upset the devils daughter.

Poetic Views of Life

Ghouls

What do you really want to see?
What do you need to know?
Of peoples misery there to see
So you just have to go,
By the scene to ogle
At unwilling actors who
Are caught up in the scene
With carnage clear to view.

Is there so little in your life?
Maybe a darker side?
That takes you to a tragedy
So you can watch with pride,
That you have never suffered,
And won't without a doubt,
For surely they deserve this
Their death and grief laid out.

--ooOoo--

Laurie Wilkinson

Hand of God

Scenic beauty, sweet fresh air
All you could wish for, it was there,
For one more moment, then it was gone
When the coward set off another bomb.

Smoke and flames, cries and screams
Another end to countless dreams,
A place of wonder to melt all hearts
Was now a horror of body parts!

All be praised, his god is served
The dead just got what they deserved,
For not praying the same as those
Who blew them up and burnt their clothes.

Some strange god, that death he asks
From his army with their bloody tasks,
That spreads out terror, fear and dread
And victories measured by the dead.

Again you pray, your day is won
Religion spread by your smoking gun,
It is honour you want, your way is best,
Go tell the man with his shattered chest.

Little children, babes in arms
Now lie slaughtered with no more charms,
You say it is vengeance, we had done wrong
So we must suffer you sick death song.

It is peace you wish, and to make us sure
You continue to kill, and make more war,
Until we learn, and have passed the test
That your gentle, loving god is the best.

Poetic Views of Life

Laurie Wilkinson

TRAGEDY

Poetic Views of Life

Laurie Wilkinson

Moving On

Our death is certain
That we all know,
But when, is the mystery
And how will we go?

Will we be ancient
Sick frail and weak?
And dependent on others
For the succour we seek.

Perhaps not so old
But contorted with pain,
As our body shuts down
And wont start again.

But some will decide
To decree their own fate,
And control any future
In their suicide state.

And what of young ones
With a lifetime ahead?
That cruel destiny curtails
And cuts them stone dead!

Thus our lifetime journey
Will evolve come what may,
And we can only ensure
To make the most of each day.

Poetic Views of Life

Blind Alleys

The sands of time will educate
Just what we should have done,
But these lessons are of no use
However quick we run.

The past is gone and can't be changed
However much we'd like to,
Forget, erase and put all right
So it rests at ease inside you.

So try to forget or come to terms
With things that don't sit light,
Upon a conscience shouting out
The things you can't make right.

Mistakes made, or spiteful words
May reappear and haunt,
An awakened or sleepless soul
That bad memories will flaunt.

There's a private calling inner self
That speaks louder in the dark,
Of uncertainties that grow
Bright from the smallest spark.

The very stoutest heart and frame
Will wilt from past torment,
Unless a covenant you make
Before your time is spent.

Words spoken and dreams made
At a time your ideas leapt,
Seemed all right and proper then
So them now you must accept!

Laurie Wilkinson

Out of Time
(On the passing of a dear friend)

Crashing wind and driving rain
Conspired to fill the day,
That you were finally laid to rest
And gave everyone their say,
Of all that you had meant to them
In each and every way.

But though your candle has gone out
Your spirit still shines bright,
And no disgusting weather's blast
Could cause us any doubt,
That you had brightened up the life
Of all that came in sight.

It's said that when you leave this earth
You wend your way to heaven,
But whether you believe in this
And however you are leaven,
None should have to leave the world
When they're aged just fifty seven!

Crashing winds and driving rain
Conspired to fill the day,
That you were finally laid to rest
And made the light seem grey.
Crashing winds and driving rain
Washed the tears and gave its sign,
That however hard you'd tried
You had still run out of time.

Poetic Views of Life

So now the final dye is cast
It is up to us to ponder,
Are we set for many better things
If in this life we squander,
Time and love that we may lose
Searching for a wide blue yonder.

--ooOoo--

Laurie Wilkinson

Groom and Doom

Her pretty eyes were dulled
Behind her battered face,
His fists had won the argument
But marked out his disgrace.

He said that she deserved it
It was her fault all along,
But it was only peace she craved
Whether she was right or wrong.

He started as a proper gent
Very keen to get along,
Until she had opinions
And then he changed his song.

Bullies like to be in charge
And pick on someone small,
Or a woman who seems loving
And not challenge him at all.

So he really did not like it
When his victim tried to choose,
And if she tried to protest
She wore another bruise.

These abusers are insecure
In fear of other men,
So he stops his ladies leisure
Always checking on her when

She tries to see other people
Who would like to help her out,
But she is really trapped now
And still gets knocked about!

Poetic Views of Life

So how is she to escape?
The police aren't always there
And any banning order
Just increases the nightmare

Of abuse and vile words
That turn her blood to ice,
And makes her want to run away
But he controls her like a vice.

Friends and family are cut off
They pose too much a threat,
So her world has really shrunk now
Much too late for her regret.

The only hope now is the media
To expose this domestic dread,
But it needs to happen quickly
Before she is also dead!

--ooOoo--

Laurie Wilkinson

Crowded Out

Can a tree in a forest be lonely
Or a wave crest on the sea?
So if surrounded by people
How can loneliness possibly be?

When you look at peoples faces
For a smile or glint of an eye,
Everyone seems to be moving
And like spectres just pass by.

The fish in the ocean have shoals
And the bees will build their hive,
But many people live in surroundings
Where no one knows they're alive.

So maybe we should reach out
With more effort to connect,
To try and prevent isolation
That even stout hearts will deject.

No person wants their passing
To go off with barely a squeak,
With people saying they saw them
But never found time to speak!

--ooOoo--

Speedy End

The fool in a desperate hurry
Roars his car against the bend,
Whilst every other driver
Knows just how this will end.

His metal box wrapped round him
The wheel crushed on his chest,
How many times you tell him
He thinks he knows what's best.

So he goes on taking chances
Driving over lights at red,
And the sad fact of the matter
Is that soon he will be dead.

And his family will be mourning
For his death and lack of years,
But it's too late now for lessons
All that's left are wasted tears!

--ooOoo--

Laurie Wilkinson

Paradox of Life

Loving words and passions sighs
Fall like gifts from heavens skies,
You walk on clouds, feel ten feet high
And talk to angels passing by.

But life will always have a sting
And back to hard earth it will bring,
Brief times that mock to disbelieve
Emotions flattered to deceive.

--ooOoo--

Miss Judas Regrets

Through all childhood's carefree time
There had been no need to grieve,
Until the time my world was rocked
And you picked that time to leave.

You had sought to be with me
Until I finally went along,
Enjoying all those happy times
When we sang each others song.

Everyday was a sunshine time
More than the world could know,
But then for me a tragedy
That was when you chose to go.

Our love was feeling autumn's chill
Though we tried to keep it heated,
Until my loss gave you a chance
And very soon you cheated,
On everything we'd said and done
And every human trait.
You crossed the line of decency
And went to traitors gate.
The betrayal wrought by Judas
In that cruel Gethsemane,
Was evil, foul and sordid
Just like you were for me!

But I am born of stoic roots
Though stunned I still stood firm,
Enough to pour contempt on you
And see you fawn and squirm!

Laurie Wilkinson

Through all childhoods carefree time
There had been no need to grieve,
Until the time my world was rocked
And you picked that time to leave.

I wondered just how you could live
So close to your betrayal,
Until your shame caused you to run
With your gutless twisted male,
Who somehow had defied the loss
Of one he should have cherished,
But together your sick sad act
Ensured your souls should perish.

Someone Says Goodbye

See how quick we can be gone
And the world will blink and carry on,
Another soul out the exit door
Whilst we wonder what life is for.

There must be more for us than this
A racing heart and a loving kiss,
All our struggles, and an uphill climb
Take our words and make them mime.

Mothers, fathers, siblings and friends
We are all these before our ends,
But what of this when we are to go
What will change, and who will know?

See how quick we can be gone
And the world will blink and carry on,
So we may learn how hard they try
When someone has to say goodbye.

Laughing, crying, bitter sweet years
That gave us joy or shed our tears,
And looking back from an ageing eye
Condemning those who would not try
To ever give, or leave their mark
On a wasted life without a spark,
As for them it was all much too hard,
They passed on by, never played a card.

See how quick we can be gone
And the world will blink and carry on,
With daily tasks that must be done
Or problems causing us to run.

Laurie Wilkinson

But wait, a lesson will be taught
From those who died but valiant fought,
To spend more time with those that care
Not granted! Who said life was fair?
So as we hear their struggling breath
As they slide towards impending death,
See how quick we can be gone
And the world might blink and carry on.

Some things can make life worthwhile,
Just leave a little of your style,
To sprinkle out and upward fly
When your turn comes to say goodbye.

--ooOoo--

Poetic Views of Life

Appendix

(The poems are largely self explanatory and written as per my feelings as explained in the Introduction. I felt the following poems required a further short comment)

Bear in the Window	Actually happened
Travelling Bears	Have accompanied us on worldwide travel
Diamonds for Worms	Written in disgust as soon as heard news of the killings
Wandering Within	Philosophical conjecture
Tainted Babes	Incident in Afghanistan 2009 when children blew up three British soldiers who went to their aid at a checkpoint!
Past Echoes	For people to put "life regrets" into perspective
Silence Thunders	Focus on and appreciate people whilst they're still with us
Monsoon	Winter 2013/14
Hand of God	Revulsion of indiscriminate terror bombings in name of religion
Blind Alleys	To learn from our lives

Poetic Views of Life

Groom and Doom	Hoping to highlight the lack of coverage and reporting of Domestic Abuse
Miss Judas Regrets	Major betrayal in my life just after tragic loss in family
Someone Says Goodbye	On seeing loved one pass away

Lightning Source UK Ltd.
Milton Keynes UK
UKOW06f0956180615

253728UK00001B/43/P